The INSIDE GUIDE

STEM SUPERWOMEN

Sally Ride

By Elizabeth Morgan

Cavendish Square

Published in 2026 by Cavendish Square Publishing, LLC
2544 Clinton Street Buffalo, NY 14224

Website: cavendishsq.com

Library of Congress Cataloging-in-Publication Data

Names: Morgan, Elizabeth author
Title: Sally Ride / Elizabeth Morgan.
Description: Buffalo, New York : Cavendish Square Publishing, [2026] | Series: The inside guide: STEM superwomen | Includes bibliographic references and index. | Audience term: juvenile
Identifiers: LCCN 2024061899 | ISBN 9781502674715 library binding | ISBN 9781502674708 paperback | ISBN 9781502674722 ebook
Subjects: LCSH: Ride, Sally–Juvenile literature | United States. National Aeronautics and Space Administration–Biography–Juvenile literature | Women astronauts–United States–Biography–Juvenile literature | Astronauts–United States–Biography–Juvenile literature | Women physicists–United States–Biography–Juvenile literature | LCGFT: Biographies
Classification: LCC TL789.85.R53 M67 2026 | DDC 629.45/0092–dc23/eng/20250208
LC record available at https://lccn.loc.gov/2024061899

Editor: Katie Kawa
Designer: Deanna Lepovich

The photographs in this book are used by permission and through the courtesy of: Cover, pp. 4, 6, 9, 10, 12, 13, 14, 15, 16, 18, 19, 20, 21, 22, 26, 27, 28 (top left and bottom left), 29 (right) courtesy of NASA; p. 7 Kathy Hutchins/Shutterstock.com; p. 8 Tom Robertson/Shutterstock.com; p. 24 Rena Schild/Shutterstock.com; p. 25 (top) Halfpoint/Shutterstock.com; p. 25 (bottom) NASA/Jim Grossmann; p. 28 (top right) courtesy of the National Archives; p. 28 (bottom right) Joseph Sohm/Shutterstock.com; p. 29 (left) Monkey Business Images/Shutterstock.com.

CPSIA compliance information: Batch #CSCSQ26: For further information contact Cavendish Square Publishing LLC at 1-877-980-4450.

Printed in the United States of America

CONTENTS

When Sally Ride became the first American woman in space, many girls across the United States finally saw an astronaut who looked like them. This kind of representation matters. It allows people to believe they can do great things because they see someone who looks like them doing great things.

Chapter One

SCIENCE AND SPORTS

On June 18, 1983, Sally Ride made history as the first female U.S. astronaut to travel to space. To succeed as an astronaut, Sally needed to be smart and strong. Luckily, she'd displayed those two **traits** for many years through her two passions: science and sports.

Saying No to Stereotypes

Sally Kristen Ride was born on May 26, 1951, in Encino, California. Sally had one younger sister, whose legal name is Karen but is best known by her nickname, Bear.

Sally showed an early interest in science, and her parents encouraged it. At the time, many people believed that girls had less of an interest in science than boys and were less skilled in this area. Sally's parents didn't believe these untrue **stereotypes** about girls, so Sally was able to follow her own path as she grew up.

Fast Fact

Sally Ride wasn't the first woman from any country to travel to space. That was Valentina Tereshkova, a cosmonaut (the term for a Russian astronaut) who first went to space on June 16, 1963.

Sally spent her whole life fighting the stereotypes that held girls back from succeeding in STEM—science, technology, engineering, and math. She knew that many girls loved these areas of learning and knew a lot about them. They just needed the support she'd had to pursue these fields in school and beyond.

A Tennis Ace

Sally enjoyed studying science, and she also loved playing sports. She chose to focus on playing tennis, and she became a very skilled player. In fact, she was such a strong tennis player that it earned her a **scholarship** to Westlake School for Girls, which is an **exclusive** private high school in Los Angeles, California.

After finishing high school, Sally went to Pennsylvania to attend Swarthmore College, but she missed California. She

Fast Fact

Tennis was the first sport to offer equal prize money for men and women in major tournaments.

THE FEMINIST MOVEMENT

When Sally was a teenager, a major feminist movement was sweeping across the United States. Feminism is the belief that men and women are equals and should be treated as such. The feminist movement that spread in the 1960s is sometimes called the women's liberation movement because women were fighting for economic and social freedom as ways to achieve equality.

Major figures in this movement included the writers Gloria Steinem and Betty Friedan, as well as Shirley Chisholm, who was the first Black woman to be elected to the U.S. Congress.

Gloria Steinem, who's shown here, was a major force in the women's liberation movement. She was also a supporter of Sally's groundbreaking work as an astronaut. After Sally went to space, Gloria said, "Millions of little girls are going to sit by their television sets and see they can be astronauts, heroes, explorers, and scientists."

also wanted to try playing tennis professionally. She returned home to spend her time playing tennis and taking some classes at the University of California, Los Angeles.

Studying at Stanford

Not long after returning to California, Sally decided a career in tennis wasn't a good fit for her. Instead, she started taking classes at Stanford University in California. She still played tennis, but she did so for Stanford while studying science and English. She also taught tennis lessons at camps for younger players.

In 1973, Sally graduated from Stanford with a degree in English and another one in **physics**. Sally enjoyed studying the works of William

Fast Fact

During her time at Stanford, Sally became the top player on the women's tennis team.

Stanford University, which is shown here, is one of the top colleges in the United States and is often thought of as one of the best colleges in the world.

Shakespeare, but her real passion was STEM. She then decided to pursue an advanced degree in physics at Stanford.

An Astrophysicist

In 1975, Sally earned a **master's degree** in physics. She still wasn't done, though. She began working toward a doctoral degree, which is the most advanced college degree a person can get.

Sally was especially interested in astrophysics, which is a branch of science that deals with how physics concepts can be applied in space. She studied **lasers** and how X-rays work in space. In 1977, Sally was finishing up her doctoral program and looking for a job. She saw an ad for a job that would change her life—and the history of American space exploration.

Sally used her knowledge of astrophysics during her career as an astronaut.

Sally is shown here during one of her two trips to space.

A GROUNDBREAKING ASTRONAUT

Chapter Two

The ad Sally saw in 1977 was about NASA's need for new astronauts. NASA—the National Aeronautics and Space Administration—was the part of the U.S. government in charge of space exploration, and becoming a NASA astronaut was a big deal. In fact, at that time, no woman had ever become a NASA astronaut. However, Sally knew she had the skills to succeed in space.

A New Kind of Astronaut

Sally was exactly the kind of astronaut candidate NASA was looking for. The first NASA astronauts had been pilots, and they'd also all been white men. By the late 1970s, things were beginning to change. NASA was looking to send more scientists to space. It was also looking to send women and people of different backgrounds and races.

> **Fast Fact**
>
> More than 8,000 people applied to be part of the astronaut candidate group Sally joined in 1978. Only 35 of them were successful.

Sally applied for a spot in the astronaut training program. Then, she had to go through a lot of tests, including tough physical fitness tests.

Sally was one of six women chosen as part of the astronaut candidate class of 1978. Shown here are those first female astronaut candidates, with Sally on the far right.

Sally passed those tests, and she became part of an official group of astronaut candidates in 1978.

A Mission Specialist

Sally and her fellow candidates had to go through a lot of training before they could officially become astronauts. Sally trained to be a mission specialist. This is a scientist who performs experiments in space. Even though Sally wasn't a pilot, she still had to spend a certain number of hours flying in a jet, and she eventually got her pilot's license.

In 1979, all 35 of the candidates in Sally's class completed their training and became astronauts. They were going to be part of space shuttle missions, which were missions on reusable spacecraft.

SALLY'S FIRST YEARS AT NASA

After becoming an astronaut, Sally didn't immediately go to space. Instead, she worked on the ground, helping other space missions succeed. She served as the first female Capsule Communicator (CAPCOM) for NASA. This meant she was the astronaut on Earth who communicated with the astronauts in space.

Sally's knowledge of STEM came in handy as she studied how to use the space shuttle's robotic arm. Sally soon became an expert on this piece of technology, which meant she knew more about it than most other people. In fact, part of her work in space involved using this robotic arm!

Fast Fact

Sally earned her doctoral degree in physics from Stanford University in 1978.

Sally can be seen here with her fellow astronauts during a training exercise. Astronauts go through a lot of training to prepare for space travel!

Sally in Space

In 1982, NASA announced that Sally was going to go to space as part of the STS-7 mission. The next year, she became the first American woman in space. Sally did a lot of important work during the STS-7 mission, including controlling the space shuttle's robotic arm.

Sally did all of this while dealing with unfair treatment because she was a woman. Reporters asked her if she would do her makeup in space or if she would cry if things went wrong—questions they never asked male astronauts.

Fast Fact

Challenger was the name of the space shuttle orbiter that carried Sally into space.

Sally is shown here with other STS-7 astronauts. During their mission, they conducted experiments and launched satellites, including communications satellites.

Sally said, "It's too bad this is such a big deal. It's too bad our society isn't further along."

Sally's Second Mission

The STS-7 mission lasted for six days, and when the astronauts returned to Earth, they were famous—especially Sally. However, Sally was a private person who didn't want to spend much time in the spotlight. Instead, she put her head down and got back to work.

Sally trained for another space shuttle mission, and she went back to space on October 5, 1984. Flying once again in the *Challenger*, Sally was joined by another female astronaut: Kathryn Sullivan. This mission, which was known as STS-41G, was the last time Sally flew into space.

This is the crew of STS-41G. Sally and Kathryn Sullivan can be seen sitting next to each other in the front row. The astronauts on this mission conducted many science experiments, and Sally worked the *Challenger*'s robotic arm to make the mission a success.

Sally is shown here sleeping during one of her trips on the space shuttle. She accomplished many things in space, but she also did many important things back on Earth.

Chapter Three

BACK ON EARTH

Sally became famous for the groundbreaking trips she made to space. However, she spent most of her career working on Earth. The work she did there was also very important. She helped her fellow astronauts, students, and others study space in a way that was safe and successful.

An Astronaut's Advice

After Sally landed back on Earth in 1984, she began training for another trip on the space shuttle. However, that changed in 1986, when the *Challenger* broke apart during a launch, killing all the astronauts on board. Sally's next mission was canceled, but she still had plenty to do on Earth. In fact, she worked as part of the official group that investigated, or studied, what happened to the *Challenger*.

Fast Fact

Sally was also part of the official group that investigated the breakup of the *Columbia* space shuttle orbiter in 2003.

Then, Sally was asked to help NASA plan for the future. She led a team that offered advice to NASA about future space missions.

In her team's report for NASA, Sally wrote about the possibility of NASA setting up an outpost, or base, on the moon (*shown here*). She wrote that such an outpost would involve "adventure, science, technology and perhaps the seeds of enterprise [business]."

New Jobs

Sally had done many amazing and important things for NASA, but she was ready to do something new. In 1987, she announced that she was leaving NASA to return to Stanford University. She spent two years there working as part of a group studying international security.

Then, in 1989, Sally found work at the University of California, San Diego. She became a professor of physics, teaching college students the subject that had meant so much to her.

Fast Fact

The report Sally and her team published about NASA's future was called "NASA Leadership and America's Future in Space," but it is often called the Ride Report because of Sally's leadership role, or part, on the team.

SPACE SHUTTLE TRAGEDIES

Sally Ride once said, "I flew the [space] shuttle twice. It got me home twice. I like the shuttle." However, some astronauts weren't that lucky to arrive back on Earth safe and sound.

On January 28, 1986, the *Challenger* broke apart soon after it launched, and all seven astronauts on board were killed. One of the people killed that day was Christa McAuliffe, who was supposed to become the first American teacher in space. Another seven astronauts were killed on February 1, 2003, when the *Columbia* broke apart as it reentered Earth's atmosphere after being in space.

Students across the United States were hoping to see a teacher go into space when they watched the launch of the *Challenger* (*shown here*) in their classrooms on January 28, 1986. Instead, they watched a tragedy unfold live on television. This terrible memory has stayed with many of them long after they've become adults.

Sally is shown here during her time at NASA. Although she found new jobs after being an astronaut, she still worked with NASA on different programs and projects.

New Ways of Seeing Space

At the University of California, San Diego, Sally became the director of the California Space Institute. Even though she had retired from NASA, she was still passionate about studying space and inspiring future astronauts to dream of space travel.

Sally worked with NASA to come up with new programs to get students excited about space. The Sally Ride EarthKAM program allows students to ask for pictures of places on Earth from space, and a special camera in space will take it for them. The GRAIL MoonKam program was similar, but it allowed students to request pictures of the moon from space.

Fast Fact

The spacecraft that made the GRAIL MoonKam program possible crashed into the moon in 2012. One of the crash sites on the moon's surface is named the Sally K. Ride Impact Site after the woman who started the GRAIL MoonKam program.

Shown here is what Earth looks like from space. In 1996, Sally started an educational program to allow students to request their own pictures like this one.

A New Frontier

Sally had faced the new frontier of space, and by the late 1990s, she was ready to tackle another new frontier: the internet. At the time, the internet was still a relatively new kind of technology, but Sally knew it could be used to reach people from all corners of the world and share information with them.

In 1999, Sally took on a leadership position with Space.com. This was one of the first websites to collect and share information and news about space. Educating people about space was important to Sally, and she continued to find ways to do that for the rest of her life.

Sally's life and career have inspired many girls to become more interested in STEM subjects.

A LEGACY OF EDUCATION

Chapter Four

A person's legacy is what they leave behind for the generations that come after them. For Sally Ride, an inspiring career with NASA wasn't enough of a legacy. She wanted to do more to help young people—especially young girls—develop an interest in space science and other areas of STEM. Because of this, she left behind a legacy of education that has become the way she lives on today.

Writing About Space

One of the ways Sally educated young people was through books. She helped write many books for young readers. Some of these books helped explain space travel, while others dealt with things happening on Earth. For example, she helped write a book called *Mission: Planet Earth* that tackles the topic of climate change.

> **Fast Fact**
>
> Sally was married to another astronaut, Steven Hawley, from 1982 to 1987.

Tam O'Shaughnessy helped Sally write many of these books. She is a former tennis player and science educator who became

After Sally died, U.S. president Barack Obama awarded her the Presidential Medal of Freedom, which is the highest honor in the United States given to a person who's not in the military. Tam accepted this honor for Sally and can be seen here with President Obama.

Fast Fact

Tam O'Shaughnessy studied biology in college. She then got her doctoral degree in school psychology, which applies the science of how the mind works to children and young adults in schools.

Sally's life partner in the 1980s. Together, they worked to show young people that science is cool!

Sally Ride Science

Sally and Tam were successful women in STEM fields, and they wanted to find ways to help girls with an interest in STEM become women with STEM careers. This was the idea behind the creation of Sally Ride Science. It began as a company in 2001, and since then, it's created and funded many programs to support STEM education, with a special focus on girls in STEM.

Today, Sally Ride Science hosts science camps for students, trains teachers, and highlights role models to help girls succeed in STEM fields.

Sally once said, "This is something I'm very willing to put my name behind." Because of that, Sally Ride Science is one of the biggest and most visible pieces of Sally's legacy.

Gone Too Soon

Sally Ride Science continues its work today, but it does so without the woman it's named after. Sally died on July 23, 2012.

Sally was honored after her death in many ways. Today, Tam continues to honor her through her work as the head of Sally Ride Science.

She'd been living with **cancer**, but she chose to keep the details of her struggle private.

Sally was a private person, but after her death, her **relationship** with Tam was made public. With this new knowledge about her identity, Sally was named the first known **LGBTQ+** astronaut.

Reaching for the Stars

After Sally's death, President Barack Obama said that she "inspired generations of young girls to reach for the stars and later fought tirelessly to help them get there." Sally remains a role model for young people today because of her groundbreaking trips as an astronaut and her work to support STEM education.

Sally Ride reached for the stars and, through STEM skills and hard work, made her out-of-this-world dreams a reality. In doing so, she paved the way for future generations of women and LGBTQ+ people to succeed in space.

Sally once said, "I know that there are lots of girls out there who are just as interested in science as I was when I was growing up!" She continues to be a role model for those girls today.

FOLLOWING IN HER FOOTSTEPS

Sally Ride was the first female U.S. astronaut to travel into space, but she wasn't the last. Many women have followed in her footsteps and traveled beyond Earth's atmosphere. For example, in 1992, Mae Jemison became the first Black woman to travel into space for NASA.

Then, in 2019, Christina Koch and Jessica Meir conducted the first all-female spacewalk. A spacewalk is a period of activity spent outside a spacecraft by one or more astronauts. Although women have been part of spacewalks since 1984, this was the first time only women took part in this important task.

Shown here are Christina Koch (*left*) and Jessica Meir (*right*) preparing for a spacewalk.

Fast Fact

In 2023, NASA announced that Christina Koch would become the first woman to take part in a lunar mission, or a mission to the moon.

TIMELINE

In Sally's Life

1951
Sally Ride is born on May 26 in Encino, California.

1979
Sally officially becomes a NASA astronaut.

1983
Sally becomes the first female NASA astronaut to travel to space.

2001
Sally starts Sally Ride Science to help support STEM education.

2012
Sally dies on July 23.

World Events

1939-1945
World War II is fought.

1963
Dr. Martin Luther King Jr. delivers his "I Have a Dream" speech.

1974
Richard Nixon becomes the first U.S. president to resign, or step down from his position.

1991
The Soviet Union collapses, or falls apart, leaving behind Russia and many smaller nations.

2008
Barack Obama becomes the first Black man to be elected president of the United States.

THINK ABOUT IT!

1. Do you think the stereotypes about girls and STEM that existed when Sally was a kid still exist today? How do those stereotypes make you feel?
2. How do you think Sally's time spent playing tennis helped her as an astronaut?
3. Why do you think Sally and Tam's relationship was kept private until after her death?
4. What part of Sally's story do you find the most inspiring?

GLOSSARY

cancer: A sometimes deadly sickness in which cells grow in a way they should not, often forming tumors, or growths, that harm the body.

exclusive: Accepting only a small group of people who are often wealthy.

laser: A device that produces a narrow beam of light.

LGBTQ+: Relating to a group made up of people who see themselves as a gender different from the sex they were assigned at birth or who want to be in romantic relationships that aren't only male-female. LGBTQ stands for lesbian, gay, bisexual, transgender, and queer or questioning.

master's degree: A title given to students following additional years of study at a college or university after receiving their bachelor's degree, which is generally given after four years of study.

orbiter: A part of the space shuttle designed to carry astronauts that could fly in Earth's atmosphere and travel to space.

physics: The branch of science that deals with matter and energy, as well as how they interact.

relationship: A pairing of people joined by feelings of love.

role model: A person who others look up to.

satellite: A spacecraft placed in orbit around Earth, a moon, or another planet to collect information or for communication.

scholarship: Money given to a student by a school to help pay for their education there.

stereotype: An idea that's formed about all people of a certain group that's often untrue or only partly true.

trait: A quality that makes one person or thing different from another.

FIND OUT MORE

Books

Grush, Loren. *The Six: The Untold Story of America's First Women Astronauts*. New York, NY: Simon and Schuster for Young Readers, 2025.

Prager, Sarah. *Rainbow Revolutionaries: 50 LGBTQ+ People Who Made History*. New York, NY: Harper, 2022.

Raum, Elizabeth. *The Life of Sally Ride*. Mankato, MN: Amicus, 2020.

Websites

NASA: Sally Ride
science.nasa.gov/people/sally-ride/
NASA's official website presents a biography of Sally Ride, complete with quotes from the famous astronaut about her life and career.

National Air and Space Museum: Sally Ride
airandspace.si.edu/explore/stories/sally-ride
The National Air and Space Museum offers visitors to its website a biography of Sally Ride, complete with links to learn more about various objects from her life that the museum has in its collection.

Sally Ride Science
Sallyridescience.ucsd.edu/
The Sally Ride Science website has information for students and others about its mission, its programs, and the life of the woman who started it.

Publisher's note to educators and parents: Our editors have carefully reviewed these websites to ensure that they are suitable for students. Many websites change frequently, however, and we cannot guarantee that a site's future contents will continue to meet our high standards of quality and educational value. Be advised that students should be closely supervised whenever they access the internet.

INDEX